EARTH [

ACTIVITY BOOK

FOR KIDS AGE 4-6

THIS BOOK BELONGS TO:

_____

©COPYRIGHT WINTER RABBIT. ALL RIGHTS RESERVED.

This book or any portion thereof may not be reproduced or used in any manner whatsoever without the express written permission of the publisher except for the use of brief quotations in a book review.

PARENTS:

Our Holiday Activity Books are made for your little ones aged approximately 4-6 years old. Since every child learns to read, write, and draw at varying ages we give this approximate age range, but with the understanding that parents know their children best.

Our Activity Books can include word searches, coloring, drawing, mazes, games, and sometimes small amounts of learning prompts including counting and shape recognition. If your child is just beginning some of these things we encourage parents to help their child with the parts they can't do themselves. We hope it will bring families closer together while providing a fun learning environment.

We hope you enjoy this Earth Day Activity Book focused around recycling, animals, plants, and the love of our planet we all share.

WINTER RABBIT

APRIL 22

CUT HERE

REDUCE, REUSE, RECYCLE

TRACE THE LINES TO THE RECYCLING BOXES AND THEN COLOR THE PICTURES!

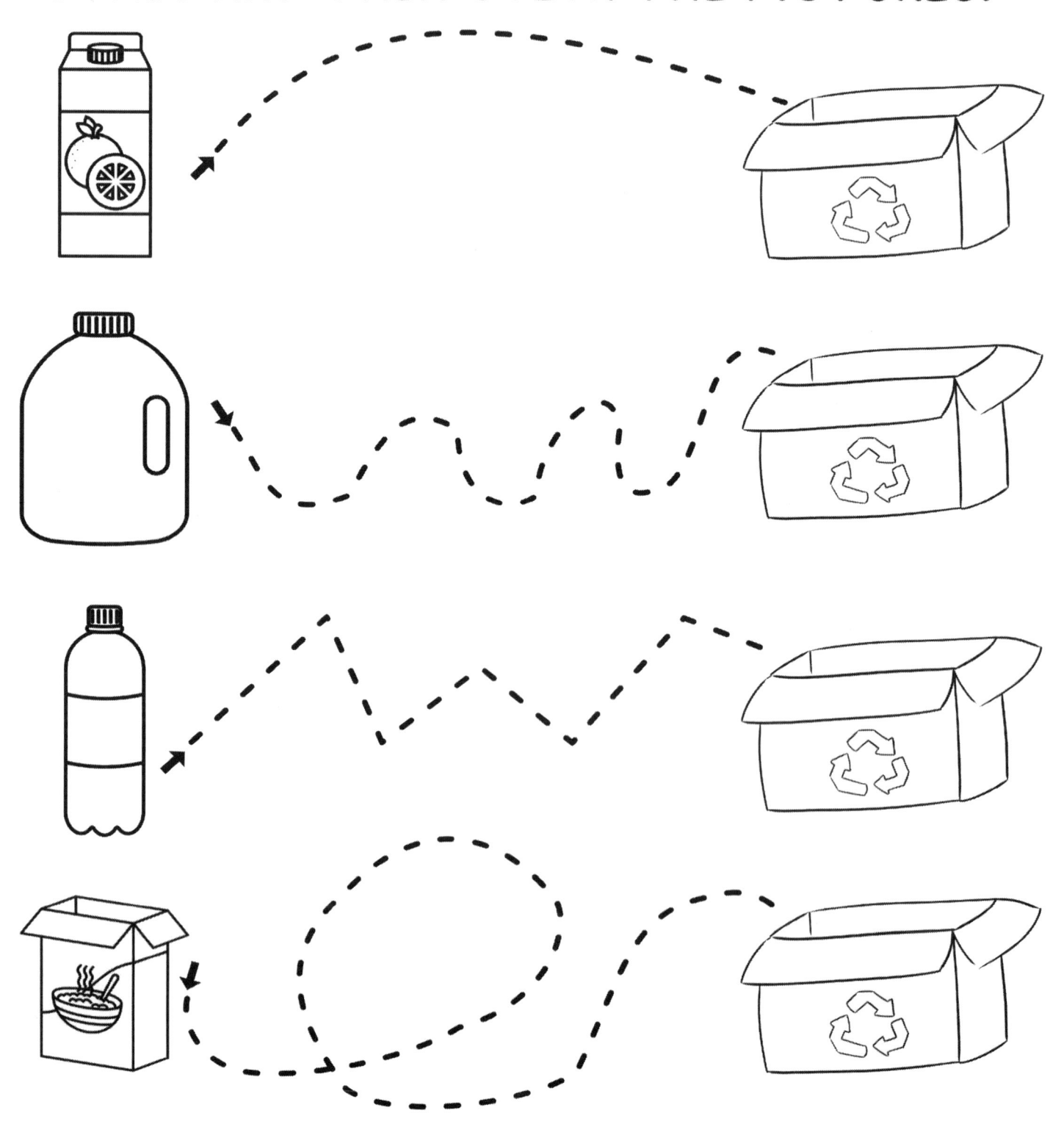

ABC ORDER

COLOR THE PICTURES, CUT OUT THE WORDS ALONG THE DOTTED LINES, AND THEN PASTE THEM IN THE CORRECT ABC ORDER

1
2
3
4

LEAF

SNAKE

LOBSTER

RAIN

CUT HERE

~ LEFT BLANK FOR CUTTING, BUT FEEL FREE TO DOODLE ANYTHING YOU WANT HERE~

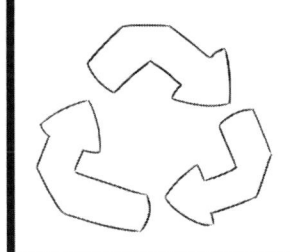

EARTH DAY

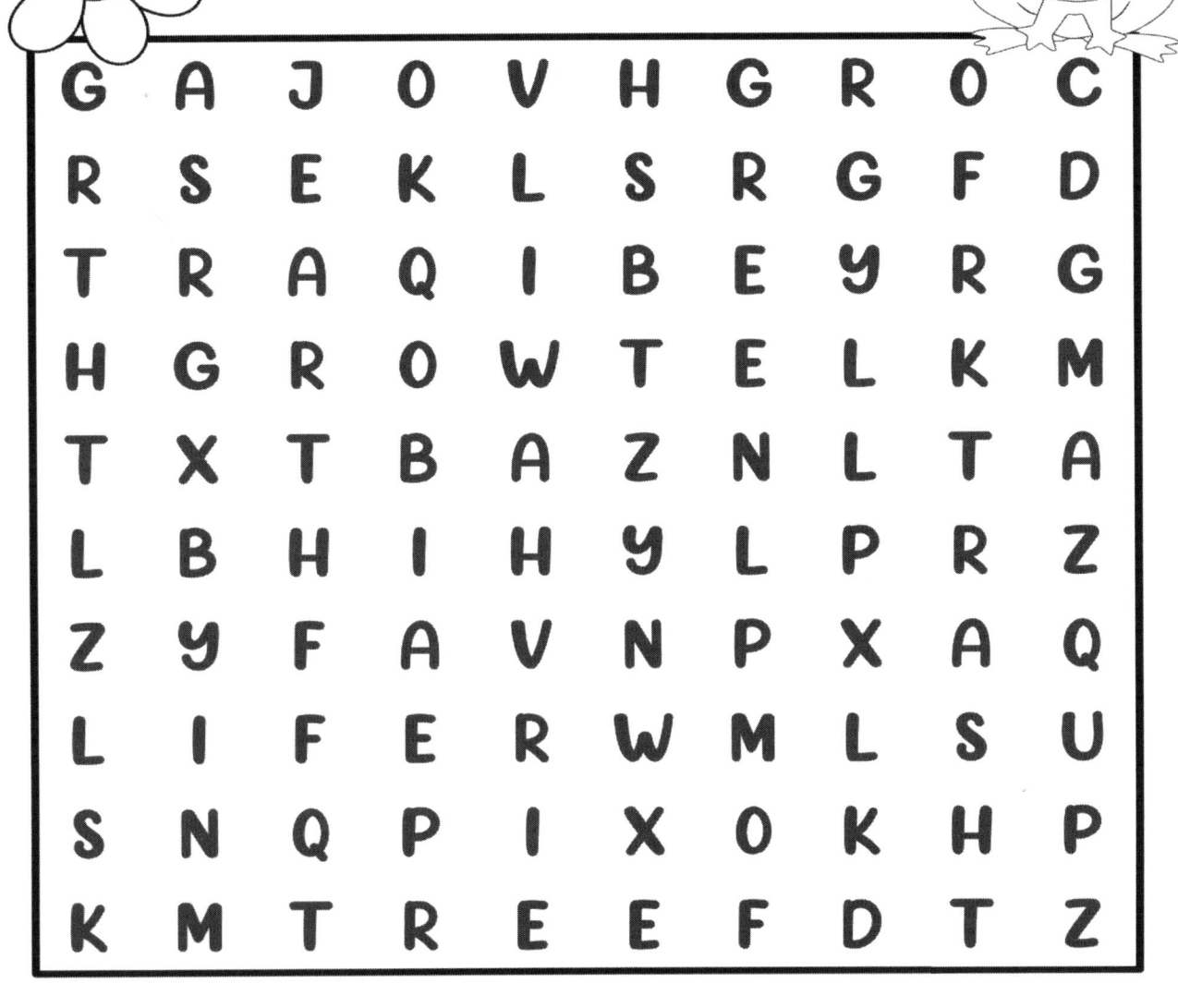

G	A	J	O	V	H	G	R	O	C
R	S	E	K	L	S	R	G	F	D
T	R	A	Q	I	B	E	Y	R	G
H	G	R	O	W	T	E	L	K	M
T	X	T	B	A	Z	N	L	T	A
L	B	H	I	H	Y	L	P	R	Z
Z	Y	F	A	V	N	P	X	A	Q
L	I	F	E	R	W	M	L	S	U
S	N	Q	P	I	X	O	K	H	P
K	M	T	R	E	E	F	D	T	Z

GROW   EARTH   TREE

LIFE   TRASH   GREEN

CUT HERE

FACT #1
THE FIRST EARTH DAY WAS IN 1970 IN THE UNITED STATES OF AMERICA.

COUNT THE ITEMS AND FILL THE CORRECT NUMBER

3 5 4

5 3 2

3 7 6

2 4 1

CUT HERE

COUNT THE SIDES OF THE SHAPES THEN FILL THE SHAPES WITH THE CORRECT COLOR USING THE CODE

0 RED   **3** BLUE   **4** GREEN   **5** PURPLE

TRACE THE WORD THEN TRY TO
WRITE IT ON YOUR OWN

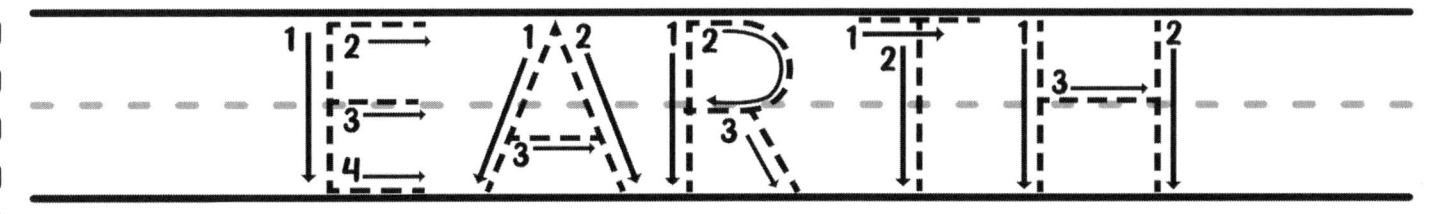

EARTH

CUT HERE

FACT #2

EARTH IS THE THIRD PLANET FROM THE SUN

BEGINNING SOUNDS

COLOR THE ITEMS WITH THE CORRECT BEGINNING SOUND

COMPOST

"GREENS" YOU CAN COMPOST ARE THE NITROGEN-RICH ADDITIONS TO YOUR COMPOST PILE.	"BROWNS" YOU CAN COMPOST ARE CARBON-RICH MATERIALS THAT BREAK DOWN MORE SLOWLY.
 • FRUITS • EGG SHELLS • VEGETABLES  • DEAD PLANTS • GRASS CLIPPINGS • A LOT MORE! 	• NEWSPAPER  • STRAW • FALL LEAVES  • WOOD CHIPS • CARDBOARD BOXES 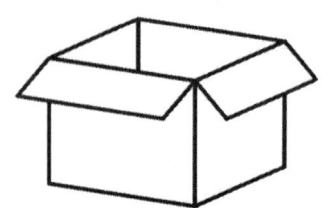 • A LOT MORE!

RECYCLE & COMPOST

CUT THE ITEMS OUT AND PASTE IN THE RIGHT BOX

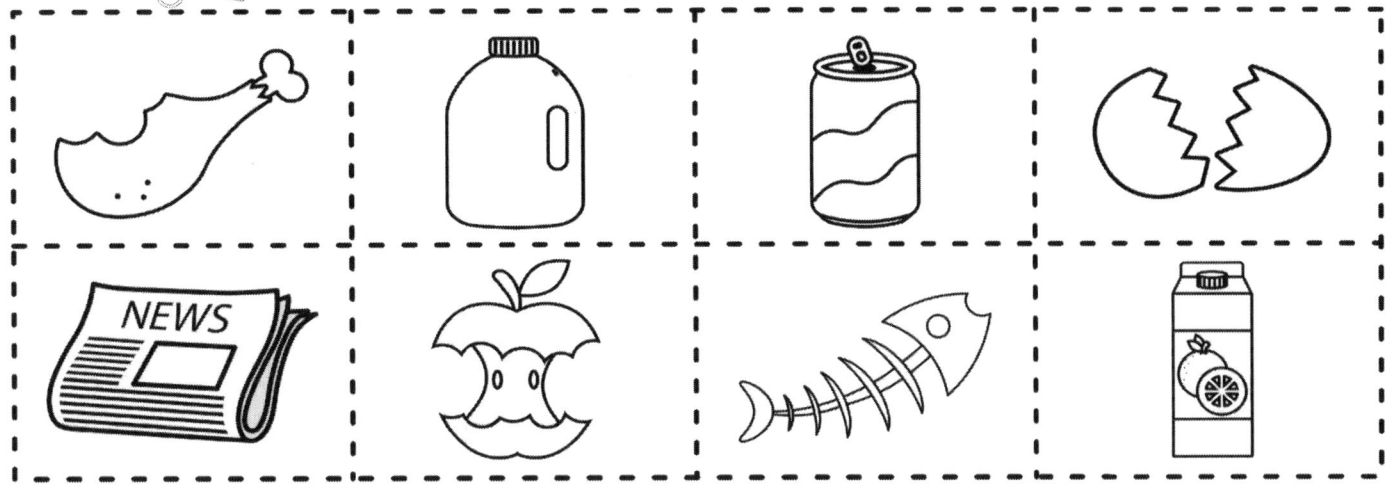

CUT HERE

~ LEFT BLANK FOR CUTTING, BUT FEEL FREE TO DOODLE ANYTHING YOU WANT HERE ~

EARTH DAY

CUT HERE

TIME TO RECYCLE!

LOOK AT THE PICTURES AND ANSWER THE QUESTIONS BELOW

TOM	🍌🍌🍌🍌
SUE	🍎🍎🍎🍎🍎🍎
KELLY	🍶🍶🍶🍶🍶🍶
JAMES	🥫🥫🥫

HOW MANY CANS DID JAMES RECYCLE? _____

HOW MANY BOTTLES DID KELLY RECYCLE? _____

HOW MANY BANANA PEELS DID TOM COMPOST? _____

HOW MANY APPLE CORES DID SUE COMPOST? _____

DID TOM OR SUE COMPOST THE MOST FOOD? _____

DID KELLY OR JAMES RECYCLE THE MOST TRASH? _____

WHO HAD THE MOST TO RECYCLE OR COMPOST? _____

RECYCLE

```
      S R A H
    K R E U S E
  G T E U S A V H
  F S C E W V I K
  A L Y R Y E D X
  W T C L E A N S
    U L M C W P
      E Q L B
```

REUSE **SAVE**

RECYCLE **CLEAN**

CUT HERE

HELP THE BOY RECYCLE HIS BOTTLE

CLEAN WITHOUT TOXINS!

SWAP OUT HEAVY DUTY SUPPLIES FOR GREEN CLEANING SUPPLIES. YOU CAN EVEN MAKE YOUR OWN CLEANING SUPPLIES!

CUT HERE

1 - BLUE
2 - GREEN
3 - YELLOW
4 - YOUR FAVORITE COLOR
5 - PURPLE
6 - BROWN

COLOR BY NUMBER

WALK OR BIKE WHENEVER YOU CAN!

cut here

COLOR THE BALLOON WITH THE CORRECT ANSWER

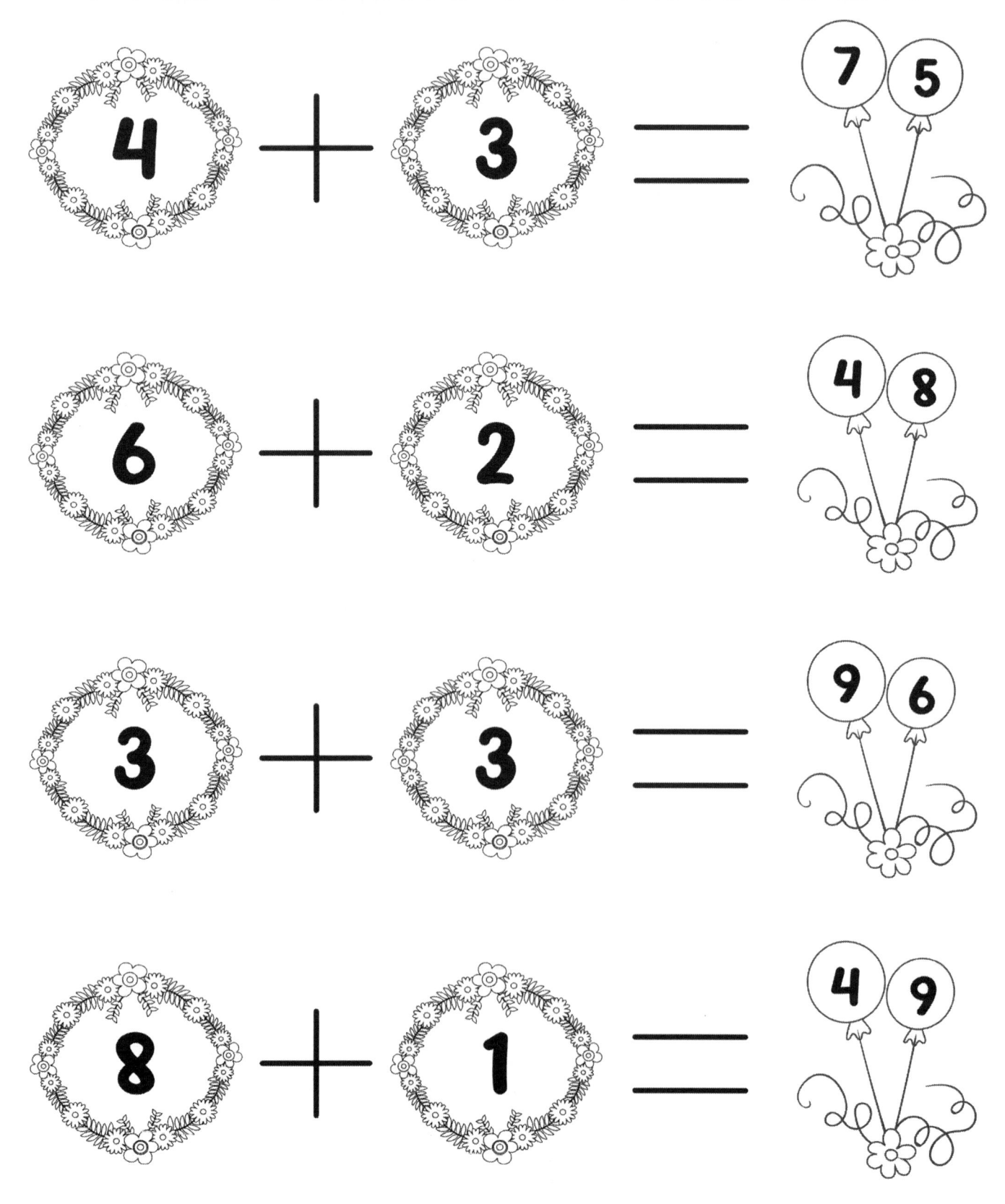

4 + 3 =   7 5

6 + 2 =   4 8

3 + 3 =   9 6

8 + 1 =   4 9

FACT #3

IT TAKES 365 DAYS FOR THE EARTH TO COMPLETE ONE ORBIT AROUND THE SUN!

THE EARTH MOVES 30 KILOMETERS A SECOND!

CUT HERE

CONSERVE WATER

DON'T LEAVE THE WATER
RUNNING FOR RINSING DISHES

TURN THE SINK OFF WHEN
BRUSHING YOUR TEETH

TAKE SHORTER SHOWERS

COUNT & COLOR

READ THE NUMBER THEN COLOR THE SAME NUMBER OF OBJECTS

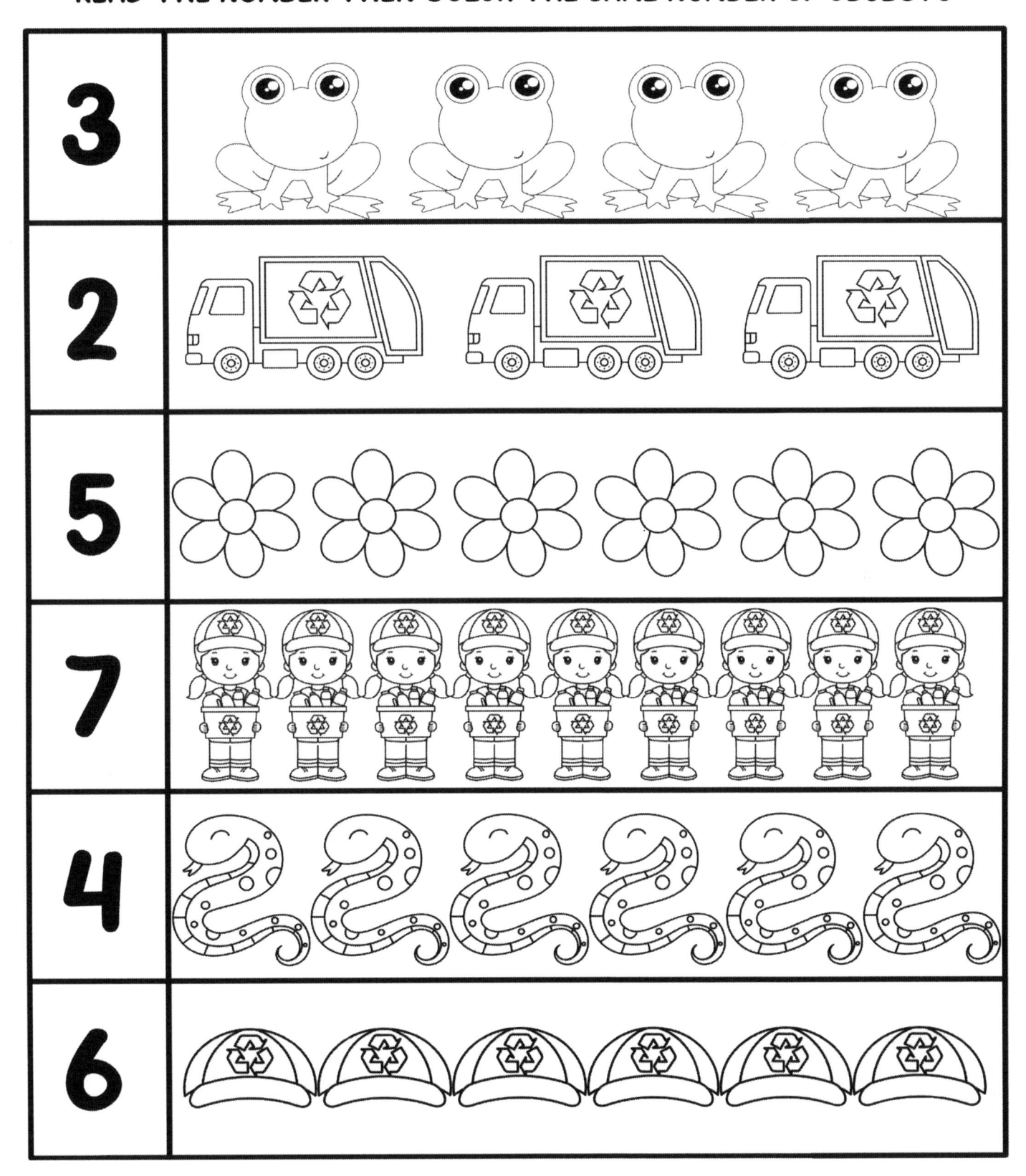

3	
2	
5	
7	
4	
6	

CUT HERE

FACT #4

EARTH IS THE ONLY PLANET IN OUR SOLAR SYSTEM KNOWN TO SUPPORT LIFE.

IT HAS TWO VERY IMPORTANT THINGS LIVING CREATURES NEED...

A LOT OF OXYGEN! **A LOT OF WATER!**

OCTOPUS LETTERS

COLOR EACH OCTOPUS WITH THE LETTERS OF YOUR NAME

WRITE YOUR NAME HERE

A	B	C	D	E	F
G	H	I	J	K	L
M	N	O	P	Q	R
S	T	U	V	W	X
		Y	Z		

CUT HERE

GREATER MEANS MORE THAN. 5 IS GREATER THAN 3. IN EACH ROW COLOR THE GROUP THAT HAS MORE.

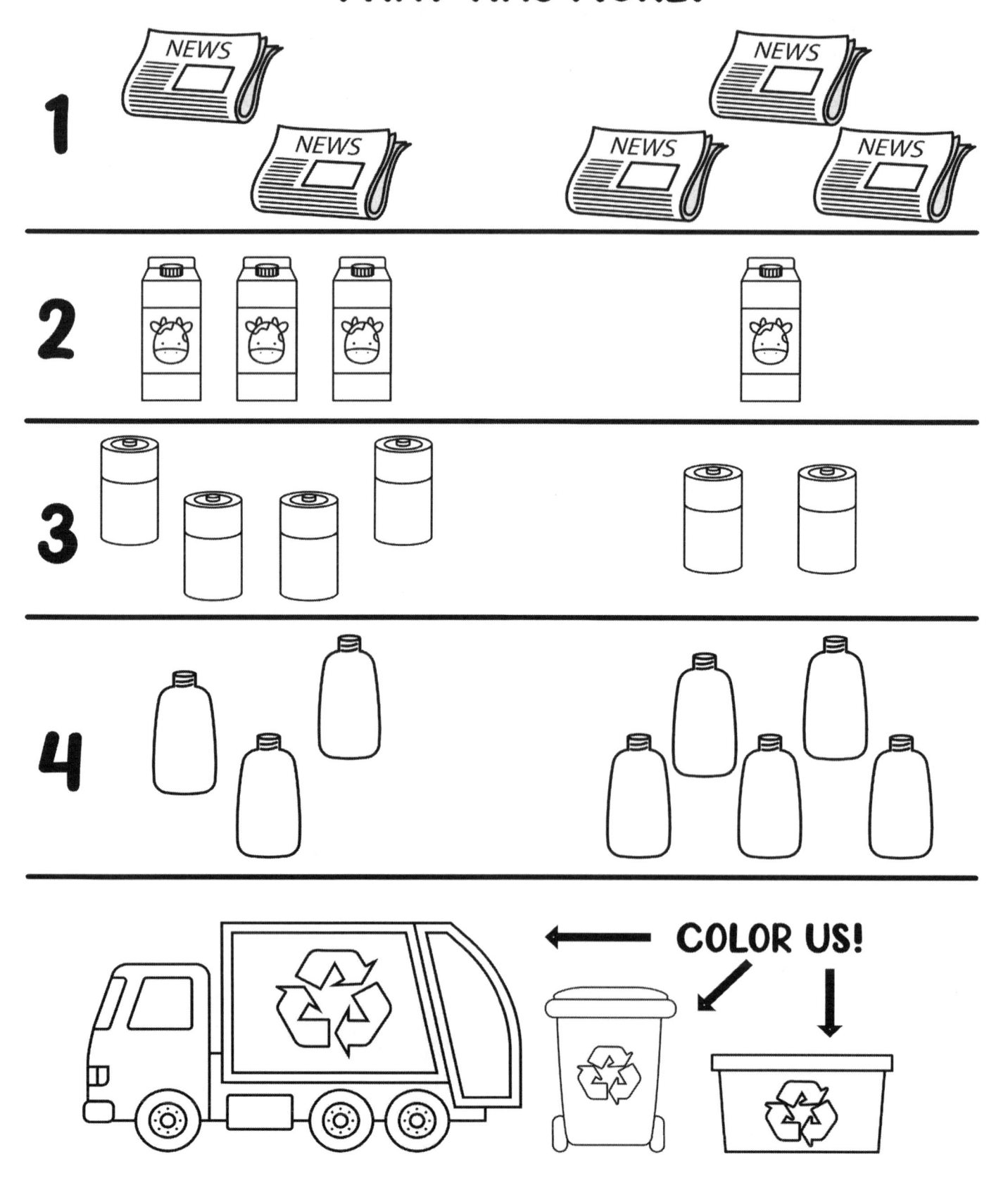

1

2

3

4

COLOR US!

WHAT IS GOOD OR BAD FOR THE EARTH?

CUT THE IMAGES OUT ALONG THE DOTTED LINES AND PASTE IN THE CORRECT BOX.

HELPFUL	HURTFUL

TREE

CAR

RECYCLING

BIKE

LITTER

CUT HERE

~ LEFT BLANK FOR CUTTING, BUT FEEL FREE TO DOODLE ANYTHING YOU WANT HERE ~

SAVE THE OCEAN!

CUT THE TRASH OUT OF THE OCEAN AND PASTE THEM IN THE RECYCLING BOX

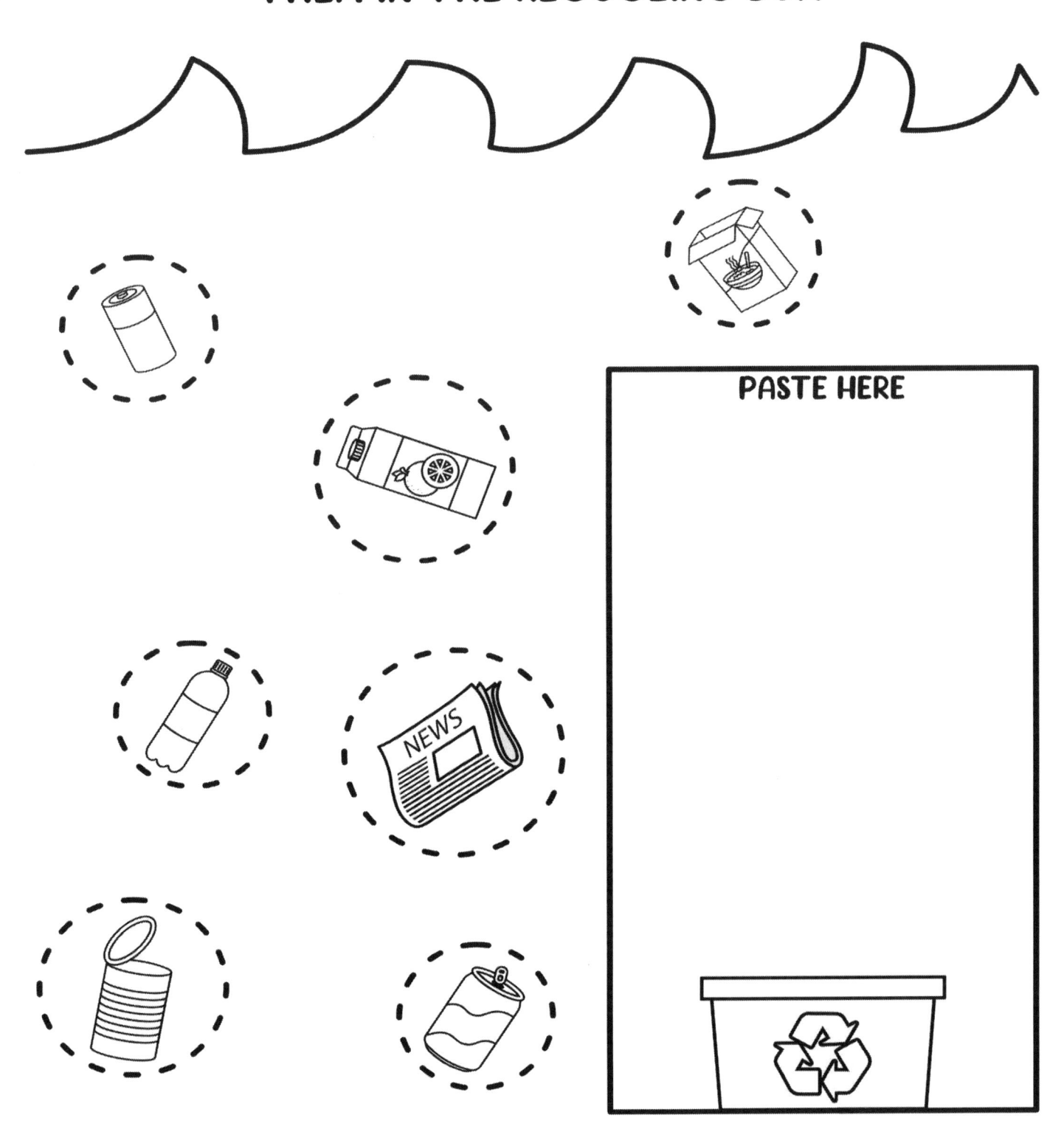

PASTE HERE

CUT HERE

~ **LEFT BLANK FOR CUTTING, BUT FEEL FREE TO DOODLE ANYTHING YOU WANT HERE~**

THE FISH ARE SO HAPPY YOU SAVED THEM!

Rr

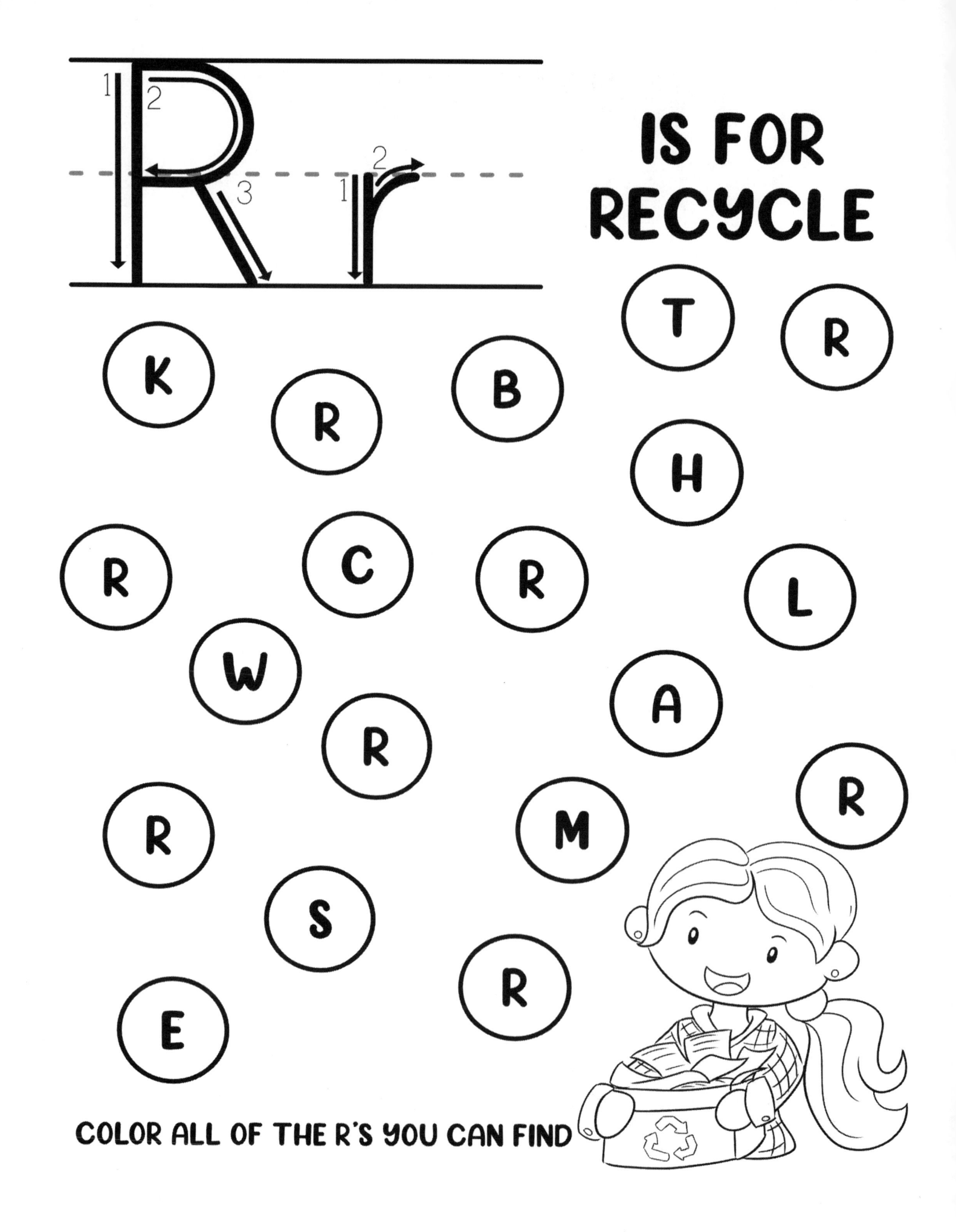

IS FOR RECYCLE

COLOR ALL OF THE R'S YOU CAN FIND

PATTERNS

1. FOLLOW THE PATTERN
2. COLOR THE OBJECT THAT COMES NEXT

STEP 1	STEP 2

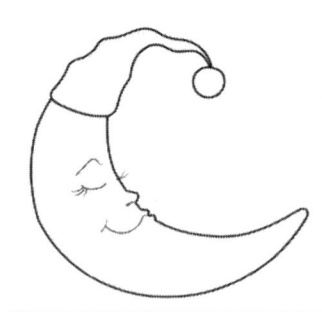

GREATER THAN OR LESS THAN

COLOR THE BEAR THAT IS GREATER THAN	COLOR THE BEAR THAT IS LESS THAN
4 OR 2	5 OR 8
6 OR 9	2 OR 6
1 OR 2	9 OR 4
7 OR 3	0 OR 3

FACT #5

WATER IS ONE OF THE MOST IMPORTANT RESOURCES WE HAVE ON EARTH.

IT TAKES 2.6 GALLONS OF WATER TO MAKE A SHEET OF PAPER.

IT TAKES 6.3 GALLONS OF WATER TO MAKE 17 OUNCES OF PLASTIC.

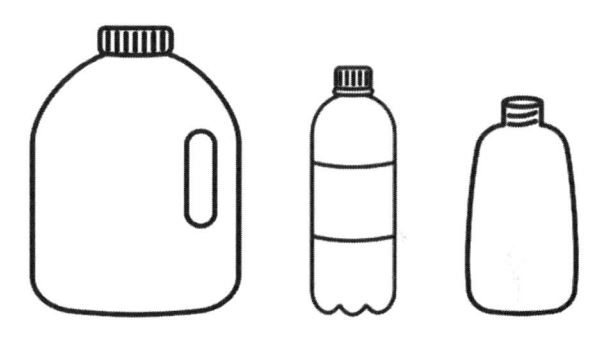

IT TAKES 2,641 GALLONS OF WATER TO MAKE A PAIR OF JEANS.

IT TAKES 39,090 GALLONS OF WATER TO MAKE A NEW CAR.

CUT HERE

BEGINNING LETTERS

DRAW A LINE TO MATCH THE LETTER TO THE ANIMAL WITH THE SAME BEGINNING LETTER

F

S

W

T

DIFFERENCES

CIRCLE THE OBJECT THAT'S DIFFERENT THEN COLOR THE REST

EARTH DAY IS APRIL 22

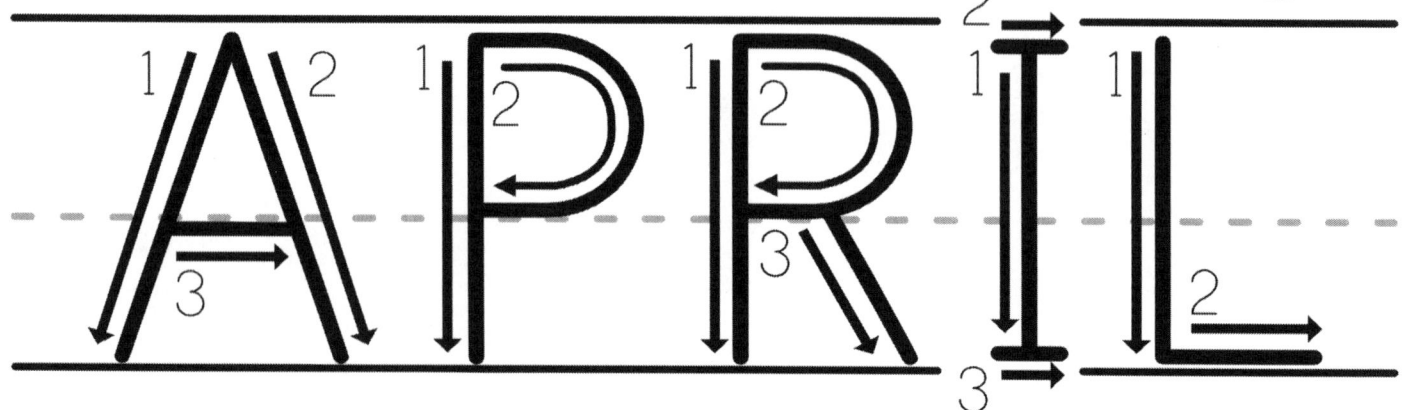

APRIL

NOW TRY TO WRITE IT YOURSELF!

APRIL Showers bring MAY flowers

NUMBER ORDER

CUT THE NUMBERS OUT AND PASTE THEM IN THE CORRECT ORDER

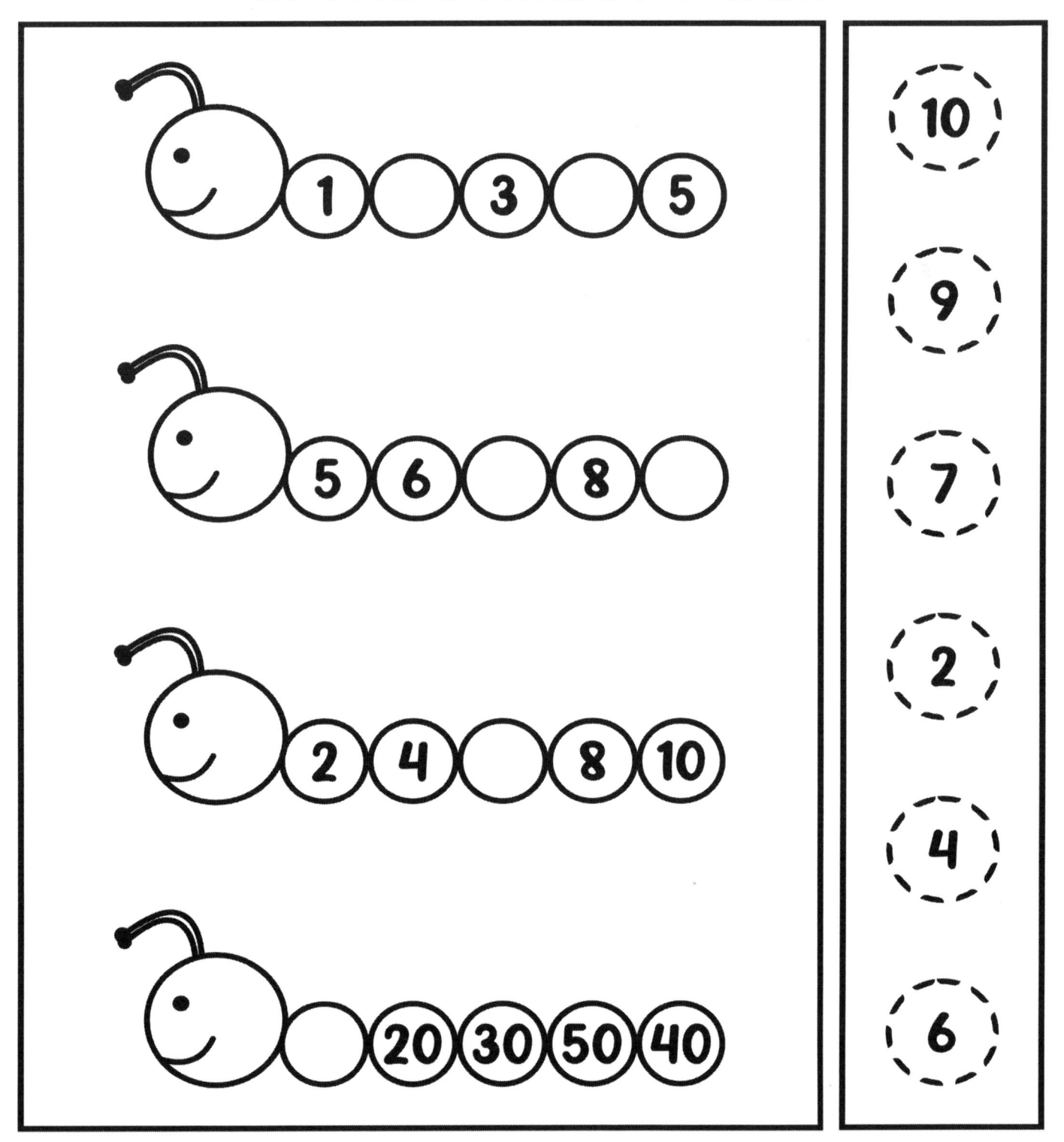

1 _ 3 _ 5

5 6 _ 8 _

2 4 _ 8 10

_ 20 30 50 40

10
9
7
2
4
6

CUT HERE

~ LEFT BLANK FOR CUTTING, BUT FEEL FREE TO DOODLE ANYTHING YOU WANT HERE~

LET'S DO SOME MATH!

COUNT THE OBJECTS, SAY THE NUMBERS, THEN WRITE THE ANSWER

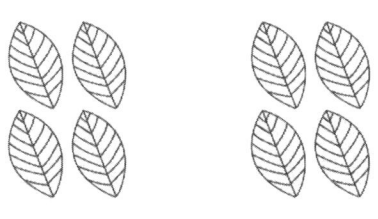

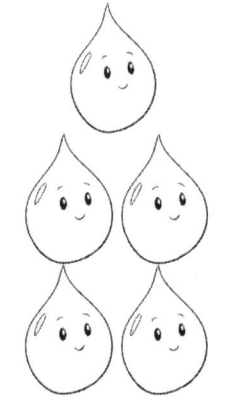

1 + 3 = ___   2 + 2 = ___

4 + 4 = ___   5 + 5 = ___

0 + 2 = ___   0 + 5 = ___

CUT HERE

PLANT TREES!

SOME TREES CAN LIVE FOR SEVERAL THOUSAND YEARS

1 →

2 ↓

3 ←

OPPOSITES

BIG IS THE OPPOSITE OF SMALL. DRAW A LINE TO MATCH EACH OBJECT TO ITS OPPOSITE.

FACT #6

ABOUT 1 BILLION PEOPLE CELEBRATE EARTH DAY EACH YEAR!

HELP CLEAN THE PARK BY FINDING ALL THE TRASH. COLOR EACH PIECE YOU FIND.

CUT HERE

THE ANIMALS THANK YOU FOR CLEANING UP THEIR HOME!

ALPHABET

HELP SALLY RECYCLE HER CAN. DRAW A LINE TO CONNECT THE LETTERS IN ALPHABETICAL ORDER.

A - B - C - D
H
F
J I G E
K L M N
U P O
S Q
V T R
W X Y Z

COLOR 1 + 2 OWLS

- DID YOU KNOW...
BIRDS HAVE HELPED TO CREATE THE PLANT LIFE WE SEE AROUND THE WORLD BY SPREADING SEEDS.

COLOR 2 + 2 BEARS

- **DID YOU KNOW...**

    BEARS HELP TO KEEP POPULATIONS OF DEER AND MOOSE IN BALANCE.

COUNT THE ITEMS AND THEN FILL IN THE CORRECT NUMBER

4 7 9

5 7 3

4 5 6

6 2 5

BIKE RIDING IS GOOD FOR THE EARTH AND FOR YOU!

RAIN IS IMPORTANT TO THE EARTH.

IT IS A BIG PART OF THE WATER CYCLE ON EARTH. WE NEED IT FOR RIVERS, OCEANS, PLANTS, AND ANIMALS.

EARTH DAY I SPY

COLOR EACH ITEM YOU FIND

= 3   = 5   = 6   = 4

THERE ARE MANY EARTH DAY SONGS. ASK AN ADULT TO HELP YOU LISTEN TO THIS ONE!

SCAN ME!

YOUTU.BE/ZZCJIKUXOE4

THANK YOU!

WE HOPE YOU HAD A FUN TIME LEARNING ABOUT EARTH DAY, PLANTS, AND ANIMALS.

ONE OF THE BEST WAYS TO ENJOY OUR BEAUTIFUL PLANET IS TO GO OUTSIDE!

GO FOR A NATURE WALK, RIDE YOUR BIKE, OR GO PLAY AT A PARK. AS LONG AS YOU'RE OUTSIDE HAVING FUN!

CUT HERE

ANSWER KEY

EARTH DAY

G	A	J	O	V	H	G	R	O	C
R	S	E	K	L	S	R	G	F	D
T	R	A	Q	I	B	E	Y	R	G
H	G	R	O	W	T	E	L	K	M
T	X	T	B	A	Z	N	L	T	A
L	B	H	I	H	Y	L	P	R	Z
Z	Y	F	A	V	N	P	X	A	Q
L	I	F	E	R	W	M	L	S	U
S	N	Q	P	I	X	O	K	H	P
K	M	T	R	E	E	F	D	T	Z

GROW	EARTH	TREE
LIFE	TRASH	GREEN

ANSWER KEY

RECYCLE

	S	R	A	H	
K	R	E	U	S	E
T	E	U	S	A	V	H
S	C	E	W	V	I	K
L	Y	R	Y	E	D	X
T	C	L	E	A	N	S
L	M	C	W	P	
E	Q	L	B		

REUSE   SAVE

RECYCLE   CLEAN

ANSWER KEY

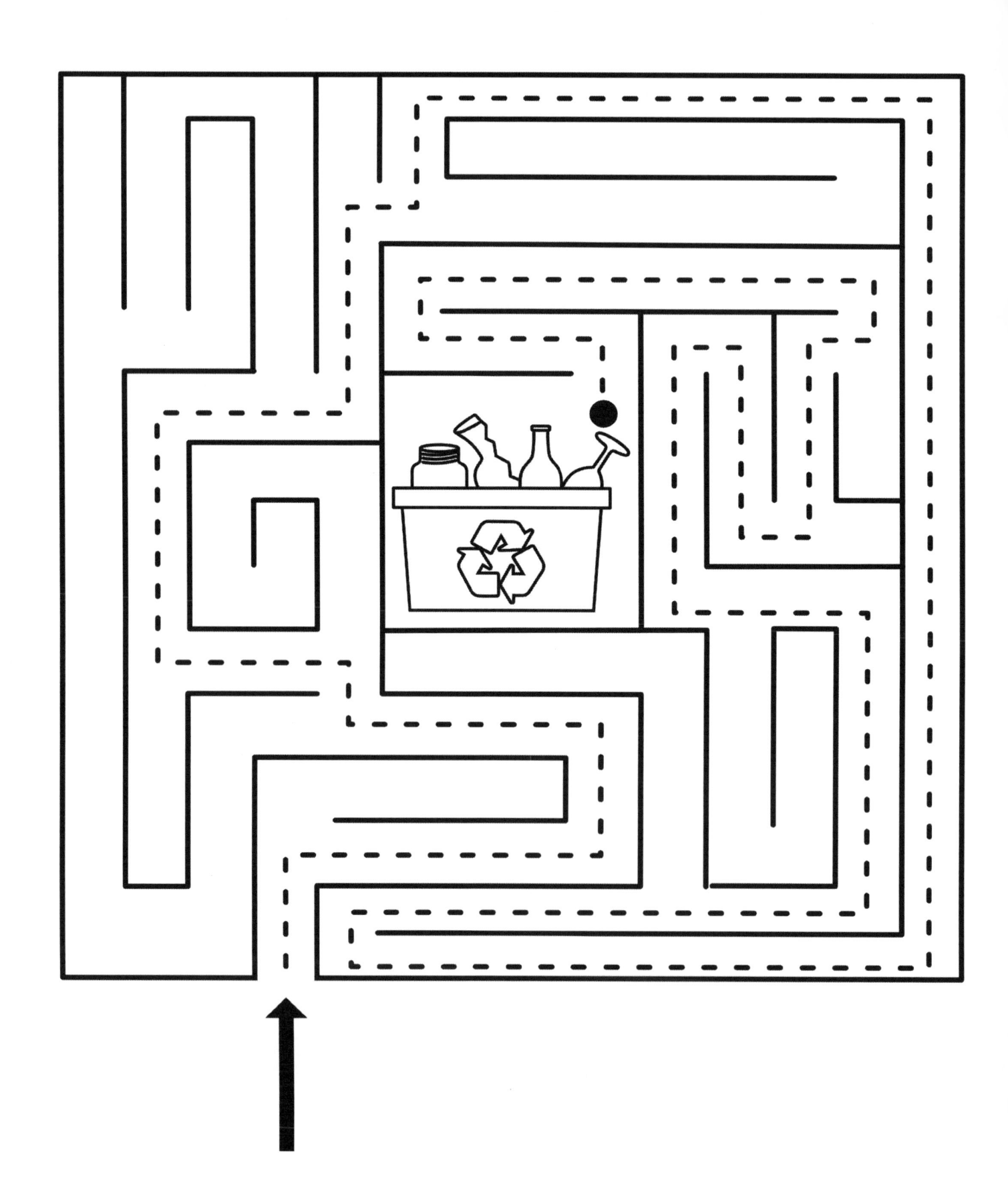

FREE COLORING BOOK

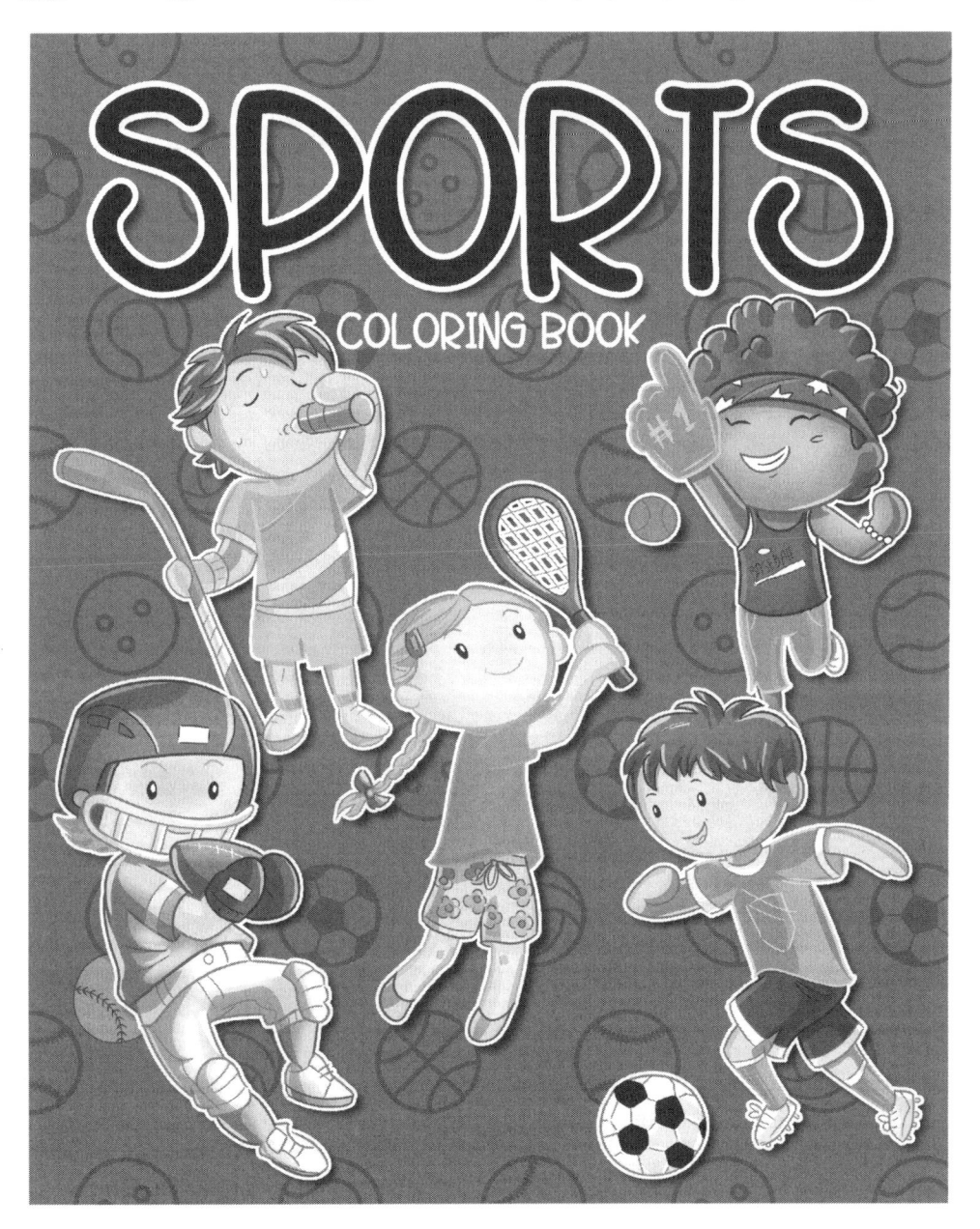

JOIN OUR MAILING LIST!

SCAN ME!

OR GO TO:

WINTERRABBITBOOKS.COM/FREE

Printed in Great Britain
by Amazon